D1036947

DISCARDED

LEUKEMIA

LEUKEMIA

Dorothy Schainman Siegel
and David E. Newton

A Venture Book
Franklin Watts
New York   Chicago   London   Toronto   Sydney

For my husband, Jerry; my children, David, Irene, and
Wei-li; and my grandson, Ethan
—*Dorothy Schainman Siegel*

For my very good friend Yves Gomy
—*David E. Newton*

Photographs copyright ©: World Health Organization/National Library of
Medicine: pp. 11, 31, 75; National Cancer Institute: pp. 17, 49; Photo Re-
searchers, Inc.: pp. 19 (John Bavosi/SPL), 35 (Chris Bjornberg), 41, 47, 69, (all
J. E. Pasquier/Rapho), 45 (Simon Fraser/SPL), 54, 56 (both Dr. Rob Stepney/
SPL), 58, 62 (both Philippe Plailly/SPL); Custom Medical Stock Photo/
Professor Aaron Polliack/SPL: p. 22; Albert Einstein Cancer Center/Peter
Wiernik M.D.: p. 24; The Bettmann Archive: p. 29; Randy Matusow: p. 33.

Library of Congress Cataloging-in-Publication Data

Siegel, Dorothy Schainman.
    Leukemia/Dorothy Schainman Siegel and David E. Newton.
    p. cm. —(Venture book)
    Includes bibliographical references and index.
    ISBN 0-531-12509-2 (lib. bdg.)
    1. Leukemia—Juvenile literature. [1. Leukemia. 2. Diseases.]
    I. Newton, David E.   II. Title
RC643.S53   1994
616.99'419—dc20   94-15517
                                                   CIP AC

CONTENTS

LEUKEMIA

1

LEUKEMIA: AN INTRODUCTION

Anna knew that something was wrong. She had been feeling so tired these past few weeks. Twice yesterday at school, she had fallen asleep in class. She had never done that before. In addition, as far back as she could remember, she had never felt more weak than she did now. Sometimes she could hardly climb the stairs at home. This morning was the last straw. Her legs were covered with ugly red blotches. Anna talked with her parents, and they all agreed that it was time to see a doctor.

Dr. Martinez explained that being tired was not unusual for teenagers. And the red splotches on Anna's legs could be a symptom of many medical problems. But taken together, her symptoms suggested a serious problem. "I will have to conduct some tests," she said. Dr. Martinez strongly suspected leukemia. But she decided not to alarm Anna and her parents unnecessarily by mentioning that disease before she had stronger evidence.

The word *leukemia* strikes fear into the hearts of many people. What is there about this disease that makes it so frightening? Is it really as dangerous as people think it is? What are a person's chances of recovering from leukemia?

Leukemia is a form of cancer that damages the body's ability to make blood cells. The body begins to make too many of one kind (white blood cells) and too few of another (red blood cells). The results include an inability to fight off disease, improper clotting of blood following injury, and loss of energy.

About 28,000 new cases of leukemia are diagnosed in the United States each year. The disease accounts for about 5 percent of all cases of cancer.

Leukemia strikes people of all ages. It is the second most common cause of death among children under the age of sixteen. Only accidents kill more children in the United States and other developed nations. But leukemia is not just a children's disease. In fact, it occurs ten times more often among adults than children. More than half of all leukemia cases occur in people over the age of fifty. Leukemia is one of the five major causes of cancer death in men in the United States. Overall, about 18,000 people in the United States will die from leukemia this year.

No one really knows what causes leukemia, but several factors are suspected. Radiation, chemicals, viruses, and genetic factors may be involved in the development of leukemia. In fact, scientists think that a number of factors may work together to produce leukemia.

At one time, there was no treatment for leukemia. People often died within a few weeks or a few months of being diagnosed with the disease. Few lived more than five years after the diagnosis. Today, a number of drugs are available for treating leukemia. Radiation therapy is also used. One of the most effective

In a specially designed sterile room, a bone marrow transplant patient uses the telephone through handports.

methods of treatment is bone marrow transplantation. In addition, patients receive supportive therapy such as blood transfusions and antibiotics. It is no longer unusual for leukemia patients to live long, healthy lives after successful treatment.

Although unfortunately Dr. Martinez's tests revealed that Anna did in fact have leukemia, Anna and her parents had every reason to be hopeful. For some forms of leukemia, at least 95 percent of patients experience at least temporary improvement. Between half and three quarters of patients in this group live for five years or longer. More than half of all children in this same group will be completely cured. So a diagnosis of leukemia is no longer reason to give up hope. Rather, it is the signal that patients should start fighting for their lives.

2

WHAT IS LEUKEMIA?

Mrs. Washington stared at the doctor. For a moment, it seemed that her heart had stopped beating. Had she really heard that terrible word? *Leukemia!*

The doctor tried to reassure Mrs. Washington. "You have every reason to be concerned about leukemia," he said. "But you must not let fear take over your life. Start learning about the disease right away. The more you know about leukemia, the better able you will be to face the disease."

As said earlier, leukemia is a form of cancer. Many kinds of cancer exist, but they all have some common characteristics. For example, cancer cells reproduce much faster than do normal cells. In many cases, that means that they never mature properly. They are unable to carry out the functions in the body that cells are supposed to carry out. Also, cancer cells often metastasize, or travel to parts of the body where they normally do not occur. For example, cancer cells from the lungs may metastasize and produce new cancers (secondary cancers) in bone. The most serious forms of cancer are these secondary cancers that occur because of metastasis.

THE SYMPTOMS OF LEUKEMIA

- Carlos could no longer play baseball very well. He was very weak and often got dizzy during a game.

- Andrea had constant pain in her joints and bones. She had to take aspirin often to overcome the discomfort.

- Ardella seemed to be sick all the time. She had one cold after another. Her teachers and friends wondered why she was absent from school so much.

- Robbie could see the swelling in his neck and armpits. He did not feel sick, but the lumps were tender when he touched them.

- Francine's complexion was very pale. She often felt warm, as if she had a mild fever.

All of these symptoms are characteristic of many disorders. For example, a simple cold can produce a mild fever. Just because you have a fever does not mean you have leukemia. If any of the above symptoms persist for a long time, however, they may indicate the presence of leukemia. When leukemia develops, damaged blood cells grow and spread in a person's body, causing fevers, fatigue, bleeding and bruising, and other abnormal conditions. Only a doctor or health professional knows how to distinguish between the symptoms that point to leukemia and those that are characteristic of some other health problem.

In some cases, a person with leukemia has no symptoms. He or she looks and feels perfectly healthy. The only way that leukemia is discovered is through a routine physical examination or a blood test. In any case, the sooner leukemia is diagnosed, the more successful treatment is likely to be.

THE "DISCOVERY" OF LEUKEMIA

Leukemia was first recognized by the great German biologist Rudolf Virchow in 1845. In conducting an autopsy, Virchow discovered an enormous accumulation of white blood cells in the dead person's bloodstream. Virchow referred to the condition at first as *Weisses Blut*, German for "white blood." He later suggested a new name, *leukemia*, for the condition. The name *leukemia* comes from two Greek words that also mean "white blood." Soon after, Virchow became the first also to describe the two major types of leukemia, lymphatic and myeloid.

An early explanation for the cause of leukemia was offered in 1913 by the Italian pathologist Guido Banti. Banti showed that leukemia occurs when single blood cells in bone marrow begin to reproduce rapidly without maturing. The release of these blood cells into the bloodstream, Banti said, produced the symptoms characteristic of leukemia.

A DAMAGED IMMUNE SYSTEM

The symptoms of leukemia are a sign that a person's immune system has been damaged. The immune system consists of all the cells and chemicals the body uses to protect itself against infection. Suppose that you cut yourself with a knife. Bacteria may get through the cut in your skin and travel into your bloodstream. It is possible for such bacteria to begin to multiply and cause an infection.

The immune system is your body's mechanism for preventing this kind of infection. The most important agents in the immune system are white blood cells, also called *leukocytes*. White blood cells attack bacteria, viruses, fungi, and other foreign bodies that enter the bloodstream. They destroy these invaders in a variety of ways. Some white blood cells surround the foreign body and swallow it up. Other white blood cells release chemicals that kill invader cells. The second kind of white blood cells are called *lymphocytes*.

White blood cells, like all blood cells, are made in bone marrow, found in the center of bones. They start out as very simple cells called stem cells. The marvel of these cells is that when they mature, they can turn into any one of three specialized blood cells depending upon how many of these different cells

Normal circulating blood contains red blood cells (rbc); infection-fighting white blood cells: lymphocytes (l) monocytes (m), and neutrophils (n); and numerous platelets (p) for clotting.

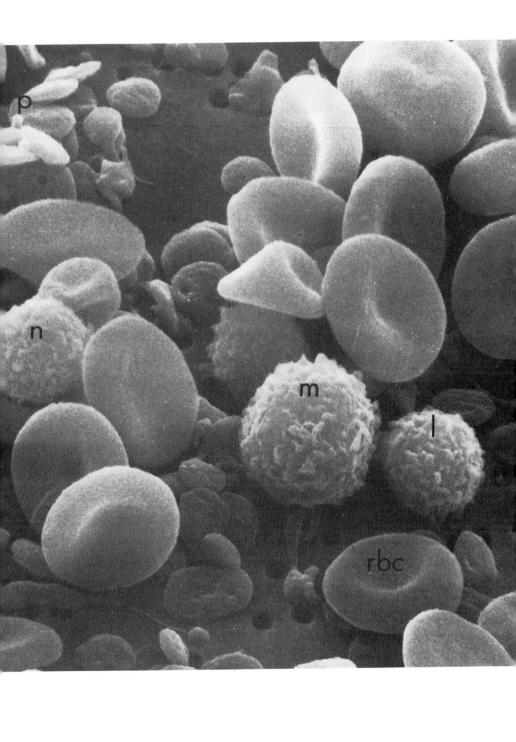

are needed by the body: white blood cells, red blood cells, and platelets.

In leukemia, two problems occur. First, the white blood cells do not mature properly. They do not develop the ability to kill foreign cells in the bloodstream. As a result, the immune system does not function properly and infections occur easily. These abnormal white blood cells are called blasts or are said to be malignant cells.

Second, abnormal white blood cells reproduce much more rapidly than normal ones. They flood the bone marrow and bloodstream. Eventually, the bone marrow becomes packed with the abnormal white cells, leaving no room for red blood cells and platelets to grow. In addition, white blood cells actually seem to kill off any stem cells that begin to develop into red blood cells and platelets.

The loss of red blood cells and platelets has serious effects on the body. A reduction in the number of red blood cells results in anemia, a condition characterized by weakness, fatigue, and pallor (paleness). The job of red blood cells is to carry oxygen to cells. Cells use oxygen to produce the energy our bodies need to grow, develop, and carry out daily tasks. With fewer red blood cells in the blood, cells produce less energy than the body needs to function properly. This results in the symptoms of anemia.

Immature abnormal white blood cells, called blasts, flood the bone marrow and bloodstream, eventually leaving no room for red blood cells and platelets to grow.

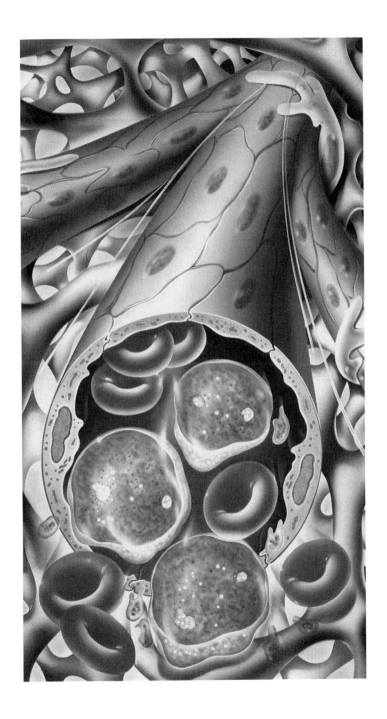

A loss of platelets causes excessive bleeding when the body is injured. Platelets are needed to make blood clot. With fewer platelets in the bloodstream, cuts and wounds heal very slowly or not at all. At one time, the majority of leukemia patients died because of hemorrhaging. Their bodies had lost the ability to heal wounds that opened in blood vessels. Today, methods are available to stop hemorrhaging, and infection is now the major cause of death among people with leukemia.

In people with leukemia, white blood cells also flood into the bloodstream. A person with leukemia may have up to fifty times as many white blood cells in a drop of blood as a healthy person. These white blood cells spread to the brain, spinal cord, kidneys, spleen, heart, lungs, intestines, and other organs. There they may interfere with the normal function of these organs. Also, as they accumulate in tissue, they may press against nerves, causing pain and discomfort.

THE TYPES OF LEUKEMIA

More than twenty kinds of leukemia exist. One way to distinguish the various types of leukemia is by how quickly the disease develops. In some cases, leukemia develops very quickly. A person may live only a few weeks or a few months after the disease has been detected. This kind of leukemia, called *acute*, can occur at any age but occurs most commonly in children. About half of all leukemia cases are of this kind.

A second kind of leukemia, called *chronic*, develops more slowly, and a person may live for many years after diagnosis. This form of leukemia is more common among adults, but it too can occur in people of any age. Chronic leukemia accounts for about half of all cases of the disease.

Various forms of leukemia are also distinguished on the basis of the kind of cell affected. In some cases, leukemia occurs because the rate of lymphocyte production increases. The leukemia that results when this happens is known as *lymphocytic leukemia*.

In other cases, a different kind of white blood cell is affected. This white blood cell, known as a *granulocyte*, is any white blood cell that contains tiny little particles that look like grains of sand. The overproduction of granulocytes results in *granulocytic leukemia*, more commonly known as *myelocytic* or *myelogenous leukemia*.

The language used to talk about leukemia gets even more complicated. For example, a person may have a fast-developing form of the disease that affects his or her lymphocytes. That form of leukemia would be called acute (fast-developing) lymphocytic (affecting the lymphocytes) leukemia.

Acute lymphocytic leukemia is by far the most common form of leukemia in children. Eight-five percent of leukemia patients under the age of twenty-one have this form of the disease. About 2,000 children in the United States are diagnosed with acute lymphocytic leukemia each year. Fortunately, it is also the form of leukemia most easily cured.

There are three other very common forms of leukemia besides acute lymphocytic leukemia.

Acute myelogenous leukemia occurs most commonly among people over the age of forty. About 35 percent of all leukemias are classified as acute my-

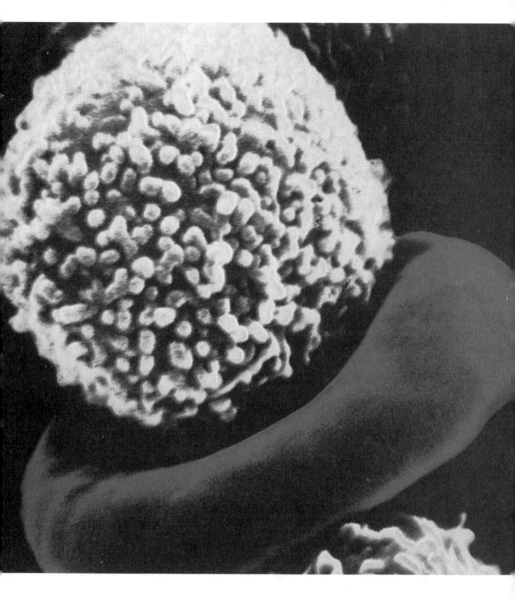

In lymphocytic leukemia, the rate of lymphocyte production increases. The single red blood cell shown here is surrounded by abnormal white blood cells.

elogenous leukemia. Each year, 7,000 new cases of acute myelogenous leukemia are diagnosed in the United States. Other names by which acute myelogenous leukemia is known include acute myelocytic leukemia, acute myeloblastic leukemia, and acute granulocytic leukemia.

About 8,200 new cases of chronic lymphocytic leukemia are diagnosed in the United States each year. Chronic lymphocytic leukemia, usually seen in people over the age of sixty, constitutes about 40 percent of all leukemia cases. Chronic lymphocytic leukemia is also known as chronic lymphatic leukemia, chronic lymphogenous leukemia, and chronic lymphoid leukemia.

Chronic myelogenous leukemia accounts for 20 percent of all leukemia cases in the United States. About 5,000 new cases are diagnosed each year. This form of leukemia occurs most commonly in people between the ages of thirty and fifty. Chronic myelogenous leukemia is also called chronic granulocytic leukemia, chronic myelocytic leukemia, chronic myeloid leukemia, and chronic myelosis.

Dividing leukemia into these different categories is not just a game that scientists play. The categories have important practical significance. All forms of leukemia have some common characteristics, but each develops and behaves somewhat differently. These differences mean that specific kinds of treatment may be necessary for each form of leukemia. A person who has acute lymphocytic leukemia may not respond to exactly the same kind of treatment recommended for someone with chronic lymphocytic leukemia.

The exciting story for people with leukemia of all

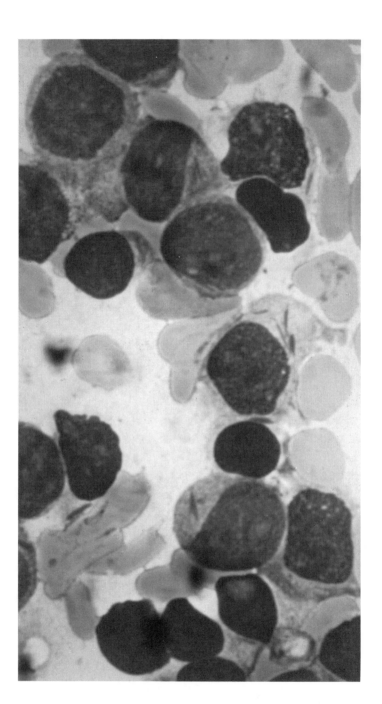

kinds is that there is good reason for hope. New forms of treatment are being developed for each type of leukemia, and all leukemia patients can now look forward to longer, more productive lives.

Leukemic blast cells from a patient with acute myeloblastic leukemia

3
WHAT CAUSES LEUKEMIA?

Scientists can describe in great detail what happens in the body of a person who has leukemia, but they still do not know exactly *why* these changes take place. Why do white blood cells suddenly start growing out of control? Why do they fail to learn how to behave like normal white blood cells? Why do they prevent red blood cells and platelets from developing normally?

As stated in Chapter One, no one knows the answers to these questions for sure, but some important clues have been uncovered. Radiation, chemicals, viruses, and genetic factors are all suspected of causing leukemia.

RADIATION

Radiation is often described as being either *high-level* or *low-level*. A person exposed to high-level radiation becomes very ill and usually dies within a matter of days or weeks. A person exposed to low-level radiation develops no symptoms for months or years.

Then the person may begin to experience medical problems, one of which may be leukemia.

X rays and radioactivity were both discovered in the late 1890s. The first scientists who worked with these forms of radiation did not realize how dangerous they could be and often took few precautions. Many years after beginning their investigations, a number of these researchers died of leukemia, anemia, and related disorders. Two of the most famous early researchers on radioactivity were Marie Curie and her husband, Pierre. The Curies discovered the radioactive element radium in 1900. Thirty-four years later, Mme Curie died of a fatal anemia. Years later, physicians realized that her anemia had resulted from her unprotected and continued exposure to the radioactive materials she studied.

In 1956 the Curies' daughter Irène Joliot-Curie died of leukemia. Two years later, Irène's husband, Frédéric, died of the same disease. Both Irène and Frédéric had spent a great deal of time working with radioactive materials.

In 1915, Dr. Rubin von Hoffman and several associates founded what became the United States Radium Corporation in Orange, New Jersey. Their product was watches with luminescent dials (faces). Radium paint was applied to each dial to make it glow in the dark. Radium is a radioactive element, an element that gives off radiation somewhat similar to X rays.

The company work force consisted of young women who painted the watch dials with camel hair paintbrushes. Many painted between 200 and 400 dials a day. In order to apply fine, thin lines of paint to the dials, the women usually sharpened the tip of the paintbrush by rolling the brush between their lips. In

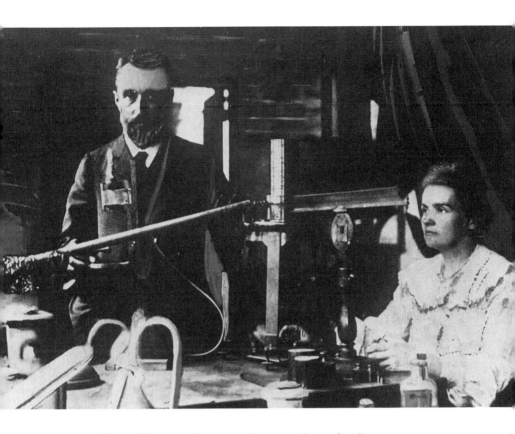

Two of the most famous early researchers of radioactivity were Marie and Pierre Curie. The first scientists who worked with X rays and radioactivity did not realize how dangerous they could be and often took few precautions.

doing so, they sometimes swallowed very small amounts of paint.

A few years after the company started producing watches, health problems began to appear among workers. They developed a variety of cancers, most often leukemia. Eventually scientists became convinced that low-level radiation from the radium paint caused the cancers.

In the early 1940s, additional evidence emerged showing a connection between radiation and leukemia. A researcher made a study of death notices of member physicians listed in the *Journal of the American Medical Association* (*JAMA*). These notices list the medical specialty, age, and cause of death of each doctor. The researcher noticed that radiologists appeared fairly often in the death notices.

Radiologists are doctors who work with X rays and with radioactive materials. The overwhelming majority of radiologists listed in the *JAMA* notices had died of leukemia. This discovery led to a statistical study that revealed that the frequency of leukemia-related deaths for radiologists was more than three times greater than it was for other doctors.

Some of the strongest evidence about the connection between leukemia and low-level radiation comes from atomic bomb injuries during World War II. In August 1945 the United States dropped two atomic bombs on Japan. Residents of Hiroshima and Nagasaki received massive doses of radiation from the bomb blasts. Tens of thousands were killed by high-level radiation. Many people did survive the bomb blast, however, because they were at some distance from the point where the bomb exploded. These people received only low levels of radiation. Scientists studied these survivors for many years and found that they developed leukemia later in life at a rate seven to eight times greater than normal. The atomic bomb results are valuable because they have provided researchers with some of the best data available about the relationship between low-level radiation and leukemia.

*Victims of high-level radiation await treatment
soon after the bombing of Hiroshima.*

The 1980s and 1990s have seen a great deal of
debate about the leukemia risk posed by nuclear
power plants and high-tension electrical lines. Some
research has shown an increase in the rate of leukemia among children living near these two kinds of
facilities. But other studies have failed to find any

connection between these two sources of low-level radiation and leukemia.

Today, most scientists are convinced that exposure to at least some level of radiation is one cause of leukemia and other forms of cancer. As a result, workers who are routinely exposed to radiation (dentists, radiologists, and medical technicians, for example) always wear protective clothing and use special techniques in dealing with X rays, radioactive materials, and other sources of potentially harmful radiation. For example, when a dentist uses X rays, she or he normally steps out of the room briefly. The patient is also covered with a lead shield to protect his or her body from radiation.

CHEMICALS

People exposed to certain chemicals over time may also be at risk for various forms of leukemia. The phrase *at risk* means that a person stands a reasonable chance of developing the disease. This risk differs dramatically depending on the chemical involved. For example, people who work with benzene—a chemical used in the manufacture of medicines, dyes, artificial leather, linoleum, and many other products—seem to have a rate of leukemia at least ten times that of the general population. Evidence for this connection appeared as far back as the eighteenth century, when shoemakers who handled solvents containing a high percentage of benzene had an especially high rate of leukemia.

Certain drugs and medicines may also be related to the development of leukemia. These substances

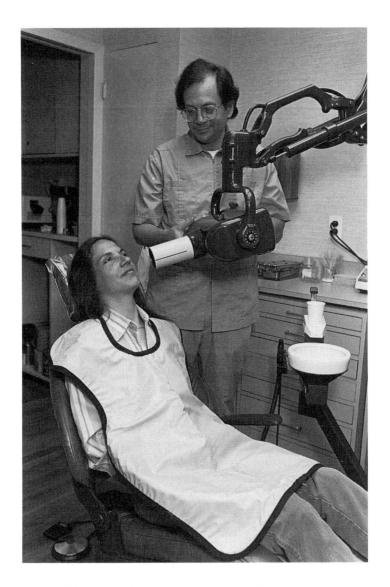

Today, special techniques are used when handling X rays and radioactive materials. When a dentist uses X rays, she or he steps out of the room, and the patient's body is protected with a lead shield.

are known to interfere with bone marrow function, and their effects may not show up until many years after they were actually used. For example, the antibiotic chloramphenicol and the painkiller phenylbutazone are both suspected of causing acute myelocytic leukemia.

In addition, some drugs used to treat cancer are known to cause leukemia. One class of such drugs is called alkylating agents. Doctors often prescribe alkylating agents as a way of treating some kinds of cancer. But the alkylating agents may themselves cause a different form of cancer—leukemia.

VIRUSES

Viruses are tiny particles containing genetic material that cause infectious diseases in plants, animals, and other organisms. They are known to cause leukemia and similar diseases in animals other than humans. For example, leukemia in cats, cows, and birds is caused respectively by the feline leukemia virus, bovine leukemia virus, and avian leukosis virus.

So far, only one family of viruses has been strongly connected with leukemia in humans: the human T cell leukemia viruses, or HTLV. Two forms of the virus, HTLV-I and HTLV-II, exist. The viruses cause a rare form of leukemia that damages cells known as T cells. The disease occurs in southwestern Japan, the Caribbean, the southeastern United States, southern Italy, and parts of Africa and South America. The possibility that other viruses cause various forms of cancer, including leukemia, is still the subject of debate and research.

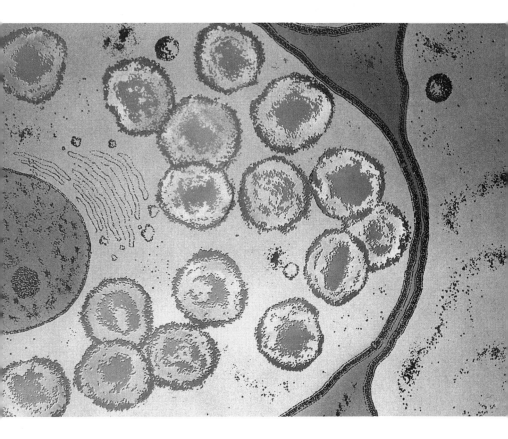

The human T cell leukemia
virus HTLV-I

GENETIC FACTORS

Does a person's genetic makeup help determine whether he or she will eventually develop leukemia? In some cases the answer to that question is a clear yes. People born with certain genetic disorders, for example, have a greater than average risk of developing leukemia. Down syndrome is such a condition. A Down patient is born with forty-seven chromosomes instead of the forty-six usual in humans. Something about the extra chromosome appears to increase the person's risk for leukemia. A Down patient is thirty times more likely to develop acute leukemia than is a non-Down person. The same pattern has been observed in a number of other rare genetic disorders.

Some studies have also shown a pattern of leukemia among close relatives. For example, researchers have found that if one identical twin develops leukemia before the age of six, the other twin has about one chance in five of developing the disease within a year. Identical twins are twins who share exactly the same genetic makeup. This pattern has not been observed, however, with fraternal twins, who have similar, but not identical, genetic composition.

On the other hand, there seems to be no evidence that leukemia is passed down from generation to generation. In that respect, it cannot be classified as a genetic disorder.

In fact, the two most critical points that can be made about leukemia from a public health standpoint are that the disease is neither contagious nor hereditary.

HOW LEUKEMIA DEVELOPS

Scientists are now satisfied that the development of leukemia is a long and complex process. For some people, it may be that their genes carry some factor that makes leukemia a possibility. But any number and combination of factors may be necessary for that factor ever to become active. Something in the environment—radiation, a chemical, or a virus, for example—may trigger the factor and initiate the disease.

What this suggests is that we really do not know very much about ways to prevent leukemia. A person should certainly avoid unnecessary exposure to radiation and chemicals known to cause cancer. But there is not much else we can do to protect ourselves from this disease.

4
HOW IS LEUKEMIA DIAGNOSED AND TREATED?

As a young girl, Shelley Bruce played the title role in the Broadway musical *Annie*. In her late teens, Shelley developed acute lymphocytic leukemia.

One day, just before her seventeenth birthday, Shelley became ill at school. She went to the school nurse, who took her temperature, found she had a slight fever, and sent her home. Although Shelley stayed out of school for a week, she did not really feel very sick. Only when her temperature again rose to above normal did she go to see a doctor. The doctor took a blood sample from her finger and found that she had a low red-blood-cell count. That finding explained why Shelley had been feeling tired and short of breath.

Not long afterward, the doctor diagnosed Shelley's condition as acute lymphocytic leukemia. Years ago, when medical science had virtually no way of treating leukemia, that diagnosis would have been a death sentence. But times have changed. Today, methods are available to treat the disease and restore many patients to good health. As a result of these treatments, Shelley's health improved. Her doctors say she no longer has acute lymphocytic leukemia.

DIAGNOSING LEUKEMIA

Most leukemia patients remember when their disease was diagnosed. They had experienced symptoms such as weight loss, low-grade fevers, unusual tiredness, shortness of breath, joint pains, or red spots on the body. Their family doctors may first have suspected simple medical problems such as a cold or the flu. When the patients' condition did not improve, however, additional tests were performed, which eventually confirmed the presence of leukemia.

The first test for leukemia is a blood test. In some cases, the presence of abnormal blood cells can actually be seen under a microscope. These cells are a strong indication or even proof that leukemia has developed. Chemical studies of the blood can tell even more about the disease.

The blood test is followed by a bone marrow test. For this test, a long needle is inserted into the iliac bone, located in the hip, or the sternum bone, in the chest. The area is first numbed with an anesthetic to make the procedure as comfortable as possible. A tiny amount of bone marrow is then withdrawn for study. A doctor can determine by examining the bone marrow tissue whether the patient has leukemia. The whole procedure takes no more than about fifteen minutes.

A bone marrow test is administered while the patient is under anesthesia. A long needle withdraws a tiny amount of marrow for the doctor to study.

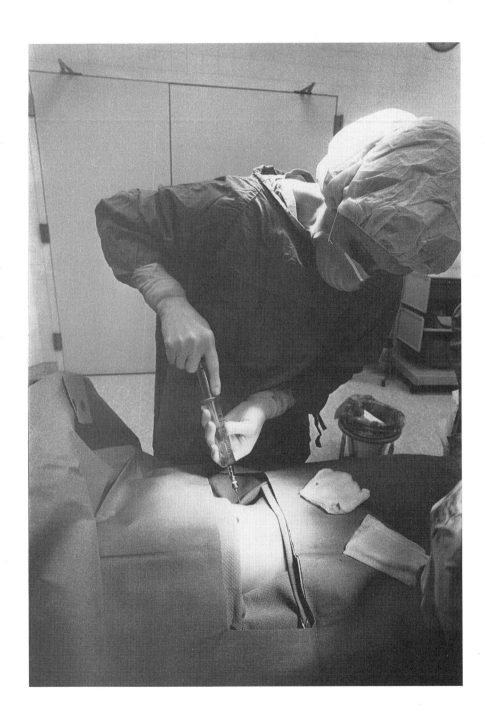

If the bone marrow test shows that the patient has leukemia, a follow-up test may also be performed. In this follow-up test, a needle is inserted between two vertebrae in the spinal cord. The doctor withdraws a small amount of spinal fluid. This "spinal tap" tells whether the disease has spread to the central nervous system. This additional information is used to determine how widely the disease has spread in a person's body and to help plan the best treatments to use for the disease.

Most patients are frightened by the prospects of bone marrow tests and spinal taps. The idea of having a needle inserted into their bones is certainly not very appealing. But thinking about these procedures is often much worse than the procedures themselves. Medical workers who perform these tests understand the fears their patients have, and they try to reduce patient discomfort and anxiety as much as possible during the procedures.

OBJECTIVES OF TREATMENT

Scientists know of no cure for all patients with leukemia. However, they have found a number of ways of bringing about remission of the disease, which, if permanent, will mean a cure for a patient. The term *remission* means that (1) all symptoms of the disease have disappeared, and (2) no abnormal white blood cells can be found in the bone marrow or the bloodstream. Remission does not mean that abnormal cells are completely absent from the body. They could be present elsewhere in the body, ready to reappear in the bone marrow or blood in the future. Should that happen, the patient would experience a *relapse*, a re-occurrence of the disease.

The timing of treatment differs for various types of leukemia. In the case of acute leukemias, treatment should begin immediately following diagnosis, if possible, or soon thereafter. With chronic leukemias, treatment can wait until the disease begins to develop. As long as a patient feels well, a physician may decide to withhold treatment for as long as years after diagnosis.

Scientists use three major weapons in their battle against leukemia: chemotherapy, radiation therapy, and bone marrow transplants. Each treatment has risks and side effects associated with it.

CHEMOTHERAPY

The term *chemotherapy* refers to the use of chemicals to treat a disease. The chemicals used against leukemia are usually compounds that interfere with the growth of abnormal leukocytes. One of the first anti-leukemic drugs developed was aminopterin, first used in 1947 by Dr. Sidney Farber and his colleagues at the Children's Cancer Research Foundation in Boston. Aminopterin brought about temporary remissions in ten out of sixteen children with acute lymphocytic leukemia. During the following decades, researchers developed many other anti-leukemic drugs.

Researchers have learned that two or more drugs used in combination may be more effective in producing remission than any one drug alone. Short-hand codes are sometimes used to refer to such combinations. To a physician, for example, the code AA represents a combination of the drugs cytarabine and doxorubicin. In general, the combinations and dosages used are adjusted to meet each patient's individual needs.

The use of chemotherapy differs for acute and chronic forms of leukemia. With acute leukemia, time is a critical factor. Patients may die within weeks or months if treatment is not effective. As a result, doctors use massive doses of chemicals to kill abnormal leukocytes as fast as possible. Their objective is to clean out the bone marrow and allow normal cells to start growing as soon as possible. The medical task is challenging since more than a trillion abnormal leukocytes may exist in the patient's body. The treatment may have to be repeated a number of times in order to destroy all (or most of) those cells.

An additional problem is that antileukemic chemicals are not specific, that is, they tend to kill not only abnormal leukocytes but also some healthy cells, damaging the body even as they are curing the disease. Some harmful side effects of this kind are an unavoidable consequence of using chemotherapy. But medical scientists try to adjust dosages to reduce side effects as much as possible.

Chemotherapy treatment is used to interfere with the growth of abnormal leukocytes. This young leukemia patient may receive intravenous chemotherapy drugs a number of times in order to destroy all, or most of, the abnormal cells.

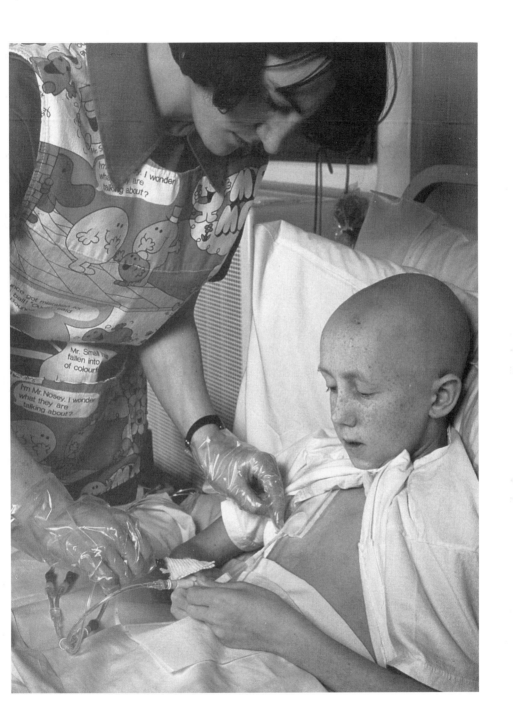

Chronic leukemias are usually treated with lower levels of medication at first. The objectives are to relieve any symptoms that may be present and to control the disease without producing too many side effects. If the patient's condition worsens, then treatments like those used for acute leukemia are begun.

One drug that has shown special promise with some kinds of leukemia is *interferon*, a chemical produced naturally by the body. Scientists have now learned how to produce interferon synthetically so that it can be supplied to patients more easily and more inexpensively than the natural product. Interferon appears to have a number of functions, not all of which are completely understood. It has been especially successful in delaying the progress, or even bringing about the remission, of chronic myelogenous leukemia.

Any medication can cause side effects, and this is especially true with some antileukemic drugs. The side effects a person experiences depend on three factors: the patient's own body characteristics, the type of leukemia being treated, and—most important—the drugs being used.

The most common side effects of antileukemic chemotherapy include nausea, vomiting, loss of ap-

After sixty-three days in the hospital, suffering the side effects of hair loss and bloating from antileukemic chemotherapy, this young patient and his mother await his release from the hospital for recovery and observation.

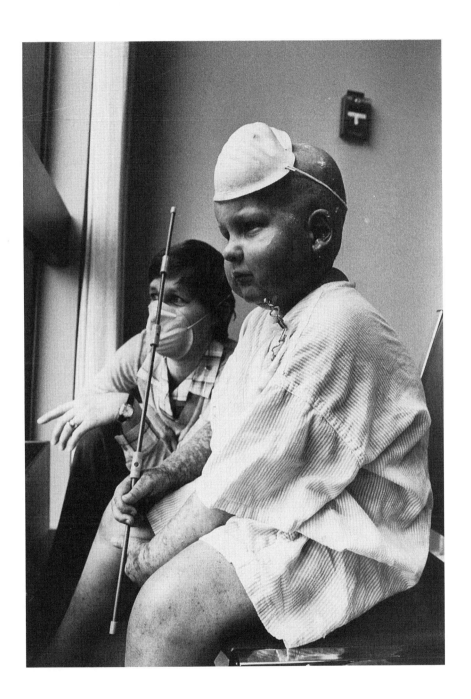

petite, diarrhea, fever, loss of hair, and nerve damage. Many other body changes are possible, but less common. These include weight gain, bloating, increase in appetite, diabetes, and inflammation of the pancreas.

Some side effects can be controlled by the use of other drugs. Antinausea medications, for example, can help reduce this side effect in many cases.

Chemotherapy is an example of a systemic treatment. The term systemic means that chemicals given to a patient travel to every part of the body. Sometimes, though, doctors find it necessary to treat one specific part of the body, such as the central nervous system (the spinal cord and brain). Because most antileukemic drugs are unable to penetrate the central nervous system, radiation therapy may have to be used.

RADIATION THERAPY

Radiation therapy makes use of radiation from X rays or radioactive materials such as cobalt 60. These forms of radiation can be directed at specific areas of the body that require treatment.

Radiation therapy can be directed at specific areas of the body that require treatment. It differs from chemotherapy treatment in that chemotherapy is a systemic treatment; this means that the chemicals given to a patient travel to every part of the body.

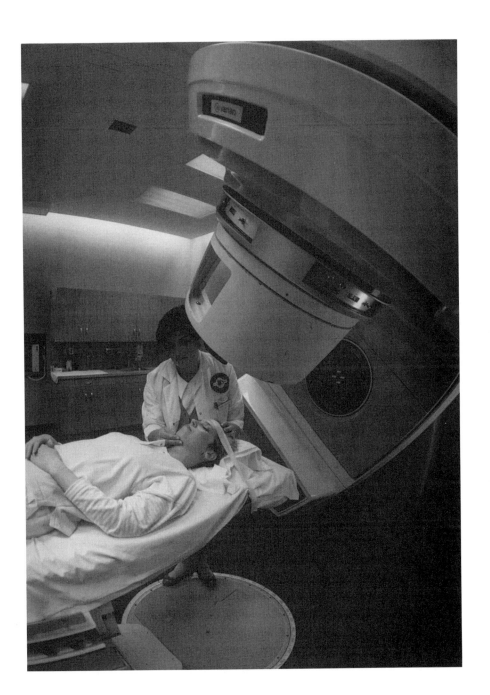

As with chemotherapy, the side effects of radiation therapy depend on many factors, including the patient, the disease, and the radiation dose. Some patients experience no side effects at all. Irradiated areas may become inflamed and vulnerable to infection, however.

The most common side effects of radiation therapy include dry mouth after treatment, nausea, vomiting, and general fatigue. Feelings of weakness and weariness tend to fade once treatment ends. Skin reactions sometimes appear during radiation treatment. The skin may become itchy or dry in any area receiving radiation. Or it may turn a shade darker than normal. Most such reactions tend to disappear a few weeks after treatment ends.

Perhaps the most difficult side effect for many patients is hair loss. After radiation, patients may lose most or all of their hair. In most cases, however, the hair grows back once treatments are completed.

TREATMENT SCHEDULE FOR CHEMOTHERAPY AND RADIATION THERAPY

Treatment for leukemia usually follows three stages: induction therapy, consolidation therapy, and maintenance therapy.

The induction phase involves a massive attack on the disease as quickly as possible. The purpose is to achieve remission of the disease in the shortest possible time. This stage of treatment normally lasts from four to six weeks. Patients must remain in the hospital during all or most of that time.

Induction therapy is usually very difficult for patients. Since chemotherapy and radiation therapy destroy many healthy cells along with abnormal cells, patients are likely to feel much worse before they begin to feel better. During this period, supportive therapy may be necessary. For example, patients may be too weak to eat and may have to be fed intravenously. In addition, they are likely to be very susceptible to infections and thus may require antibiotic treatments. Also, they may require transfusions of red blood cells or platelets (or both) to control bleeding and overcome anemia. In many cases, however, patients are soon well enough to complete induction therapy on an outpatient basis.

Induction therapy is followed by consolidation therapy. Research has shown that abnormal leukocytes may remain in the body even after induction has brought about remission. The presence of even a single abnormal leukocyte can be dangerous since that one cell can eventually begin to reproduce and cause a relapse of the disease.

Consolidation therapy involves another series of chemotherapy or radiation therapy treatments (or both). With chemotherapy, the same or different drugs may be used, usually in high doses. Again, with either chemotherapy or radiation therapy, the patient will have to spend time in the hospital. But the stay is usually shorter, and the patient is likely to experience fewer and less severe side effects.

Maintenance therapy consists of treatment with drugs that can be taken orally or by injection in moderate doses. A patient often has few or no side effects and can go to work or school and lead a fairly normal life while undergoing treatment. Maintenance therapy usually lasts six months to three years.

BONE MARROW TRANSPLANTS

A third form of treatment for leukemia is bone marrow transplantation. Bone marrow transplantation, often the most effective way of treating most forms of leukemia, is also often the most dangerous.

The first step in a bone marrow transplant is to treat the patient with massive doses of chemotherapy, often accompanied by radiation therapy. The doses are much higher than those used for standard chemotherapy and radiation treatments of leukemia. The purpose of this approach is to destroy all of the patient's bone marrow tissue, both healthy and diseased. If this can be accomplished, normal, healthy bone marrow tissue may be able to start growing again.

If bone marrow transplantation were stopped at this stage, the body would be unable to make white blood cells to fight infection, red blood cells to transport oxygen, and platelets to stop bleeding. As a result, the patient would quickly die. Therefore, in the second stage of bone marrow transplantation, new and healthy bone marrow tissue cells are injected into the patient's bloodstream. If all goes well, the injected cells will begin to fill up the patient's bone marrow and start producing normal, healthy blood cells.

Where do the healthy bone marrow cells come from? The answer to that question is the key to a successful bone marrow transplant. In bone marrow transplants, the patient is actually receiving a new immune system. The injected bone marrow cells that make up that new immune system may identify the recipient—that is, the patient—as a foreign body. The new cells may launch an attack against the patient's own cells, the *host cells*, producing a condition known as *graft-versus-host disease*.

Another condition can be equally serious. Host cells may recognize transplanted cells as foreign bodies and start to destroy them. The patient's own body may itself reject the transplanted cells. In either case, the patient's health is threatened by the battle between donor cells and host cells that takes place.

BONE MARROW TRANSPLANTATION DONORS

These problems can be reduced by finding a donor whose blood cells are similar to those of the patient. Then, the transplanted cells and the host cells are less likely to launch an attack on each other. The problem is that finding an exact match between donor and patient is difficult. The blood cells of unrelated people are usually far too different to be usable in transplants.

One solution is to use the patient's own bone marrow cells. Sometimes he or she has enough healthy cells to be used in a bone marrow transplantation. In the process known as *autologous transplant*, a portion of the patient's bone marrow is removed during an early phase of the illness or when the patient is in remission. Medical scientists examine the marrow to be sure that all cancer cells are absent when the marrow is removed. The marrow is then treated, frozen, and stored until needed for the transplant. This technique is usually followed in patients with one of the acute forms of leukemia.

Another approach is to use bone marrow cells from an identical twin. Identical twins have exactly the same kind of blood cells. In a syngeneic trans-

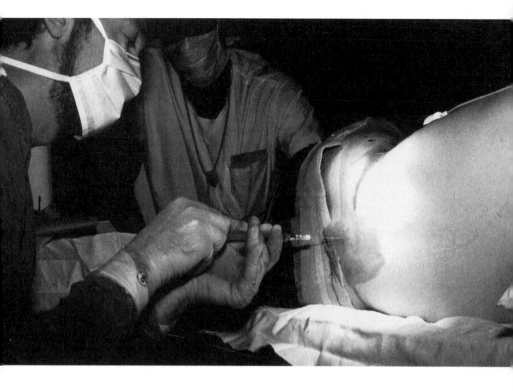

This young woman receives an injection of anticancer drug immediately after the removal of bone marrow from her pelvis, withdrawn as a safeguard against the failure of transplanted donor cells. If her body rejects the transplant, her own bone marrow can be used as a backup.

plant, bone marrow cells are transplanted from the healthy identical twin to the twin with leukemia. The problem with *this* approach is that identical twins are quite rare, occurring in only one of every 270 births. In other words, relatively few persons with leukemia will have an identical twin to turn to for a transplant.

A third possibility is to transplant bone marrow cells from a close relative or from someone who is unrelated but has similar blood cells. In such cases, the match between donor and host will be inexact, but may be close enough to reduce the risk of rejection to an acceptable level. This kind of transplant is known as allogeneic transplant, or allogeneic graft.

The success of an allogeneic transplant depends largely on how closely the donated marrow matches the patient's own marrow. Such a matching process involves locating special cell characteristics known as *antigens*. Scientists study the characteristics called human leukocyte antigens attached to blood cells to judge whether a potential donor and the recipient share any of those antigens. The chances of a successful transplant increase with the number of matches. Experts feel that there should be a match on at least three antigens.

Only about 30 to 40 percent of patients have a human leukocyte antigen-matched relative, so the odds of finding human leukocyte antigen-compatible marrow from an unrelated donor are slim. The National Bone Marrow Donor Registry estimates that they range from 1 in 10,000 to 1 in 20,000. That's the reason the National Bone Marrow Donor Registry was formed. It tries to improve the chances that a patient will find a suitable donor. The program coordinates searches among donors and transplant centers throughout the United States and elsewhere, entering its findings in a central computer file. Upon receiving requests for bone marrow donors, the National Bone Marrow Donor Registry searches its file for a match and then coordinates additional testing of donors and helps with transplant arrangements.

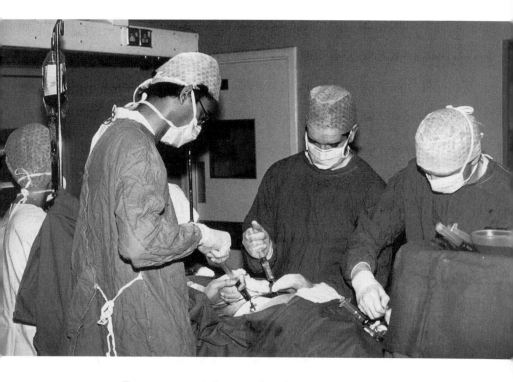

Bone marrow is being taken from the donor, who is the recipient's brother. In this type of transplant, known as allogenic transplant, the match between donor and host will be inexact, but may be close enough to reduce the risk of rejection.

BONE MARROW TRANSPLANTATION PROCEDURE

Bone marrow transplantation involves several steps. In the first step, the patient undergoes laboratory and diagnostic tests over several days. Usually, an intravenous catheter—a long, thin tube—is inserted into a large chest vein and secured in place. The catheter acts as a doorway to the body. It allows the introduction into the bloodstream of not only blood products, antibiotics, and other drugs, but also nutrients and, eventually, the new bone marrow cells. It also provides a way of withdrawing blood samples. Thus, its use eliminates the need for repeated injections.

Donors enter the hospital either the day before or the actual day of the donation. The procedure itself is relatively painless for both donor and recipient. Both are usually under general anesthesia during the process. The donor may be somewhat sore for a brief period after the procedure has been completed.

Typically, marrow is removed from the donor's pelvic area through four to eight small incisions. A special syringe is used to extract cells from the pelvic bones. After the material is strained in a purification process, it is injected ("infused") through the catheter, much like the process used in a blood transfusion. The injected marrow travels through the bloodstream to the interior of the body's major bones. There, it starts manufacturing healthy new white blood cells, red blood cells, and platelets.

Specialists continually test the patient to confirm that the marrow is growing and that abnormal leukocytes have not begun to return. Following the transplant procedure, patients routinely receive drugs such as methotrexate and cyclosporine. These drugs reduce the risk of graft-versus-host disease and rejection by host cells. They help cleanse the donor marrow of cells that are the major source of immune attack on the patient's system. Drugs are also used prior to transplantation to cleanse the donor marrow of disease-causing cells. Prior treatment—a process known as purging—is an even more efficient way of

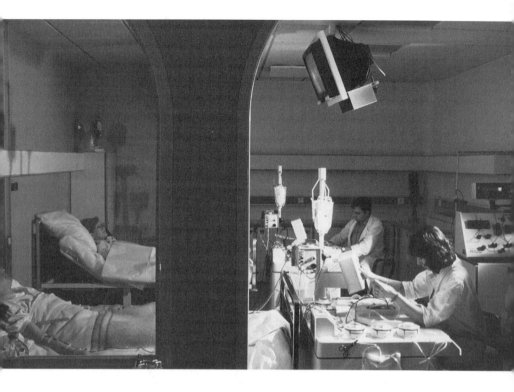

*Bone marrow transplant patients are monitored
while receiving infusions of donor marrow.*

preventing infection than is posttransplant treatment, as it ensures that the donor marrow is "clean."

BONE MARROW TRANSPLANTATION FOLLOW-UP

Transplanted bone marrow cells do not begin to function until three to four weeks after transplantation. Until that time, the patient's body is producing virtually no white blood cells, red blood cells, or platelets and is dependent on medical care for protection against infections, excessive bleeding, anemia, and other medical problems. In addition, the patient may have to receive drugs that will reduce the risk of graft-versus-host disease or other rejection problems.

The success of the bone marrow transplantation procedure greatly depends on the type of leukemia being treated and the patient's age. With acute lymphocytic leukemia, for example, disease-free survival occurs in about 45 percent of children and 35 percent of adults who have the procedure during their first or second remission. With chronic myelogenous leukemia patients who have been given autologous transplants, however, the success rate is only 10 to 20 percent. Generally speaking, the procedure has a greater chance of success in younger patients.

FUTURE TREATMENTS

Progress in bringing leukemia under control has been dramatic in the past twenty years. Scientists predict that such progress will continue and accelerate in the future. Research today is focused on finding drugs that are safer and more effective, and on improving the supportive therapy used to counteract the complications accompanying chemotherapy and radiation therapy.

5

LIVING WITH LEUKEMIA

"I had my future all planned, and it didn't include getting sick. Guess I need to change my plans a little, or postpone them a few years."

"I feel left out when I see kids walking home from school holding hands. I don't know when I'll have a girl-friend—especially now."

"One way I get through a bad day is to daydream. I dream about the future and think about my friends and things that have happened in the past."

SOME LEUKEMIA STORIES

Every person who has leukemia has a special story to tell. Those stories are not about white blood cells, red blood cells, or platelets; they are about what it's like to be living with leukemia. And they are as different as the people who tell them.

BROOKE WARD
Brooke Ward was born on Valentine's Day, 1981, in Chapel Hill, North Carolina. She was a bright,

A young transplant patient

bouncy little girl. But shortly before her third birthday, she started to become subdued and listless and developed persistent flulike symptoms.

Naturally, her parents were concerned. Mrs. Ward took Brooke to their family doctor, then to several specialists. The doctors all agreed on the diagnosis: Brooke had acute lymphatic leukemia. Within days, she began treatment for the disease.

Monthly, for two years, Brooke and her mother traveled to the University of North Carolina Memorial Hospital in Chapel Hill for chemotherapy. Brooke never complained. On the contrary, she was extraordinarily brave. At the end of this grueling schedule of treatment, she went into remission. It did not last. Some six months later, she had a relapse and her chances of full recovery decreased.

At that point, Brooke's doctors began to consider a possible bone marrow transplant. After testing her family, they could not find a good tissue match. What followed was another round of chemotherapy, a second remission, and a second relapse. Now, a bone marrow transplant seemed the only answer. Brooke's parents turned to the Fred Hutchinson Cancer Research Center in Seattle for the procedure. At the time, the Hutchinson Center was the most experienced such facility in the United States.

The Hutchinson Center sent a description of Brooke's tissue details to the National Bone Marrow Donor Registry, headquartered in St. Paul, Minnesota, which had just become operational. The National Bone Marrow Donor Registry maintains a list of potential bone marrow donors. Brooke was the Registry's first client. Its computer came up with one perfect match, Diane Walter of Milwaukee, Wisconsin. A grandmother of four, Ms. Walter had lost her husband to cancer ten years earlier and was happy to donate. A sample of her bone marrow was removed and transported overnight to Seattle.

The transplant took place on December 15, 1987. A few days later, Brooke began having serious side effects, including a 104-degree fever and fluid buildup in her lungs. Her heart doubled in size, and she was moved into intensive care three days before Christmas.

Then came what her family now refers to as a miracle. On Christmas morning, the sparkle returned to Brooke's eyes. Within days, her fever began to drop, her heart returned to normal size, and her lungs cleared. She had been restored to health by Ms. Walter's bone marrow donation.

SHELLEY BRUCE

Another example of courage in the face of leukemia is 17-year-old Shelley Bruce. When she first learned that she had acute lymphocytic leukemia, Shelley just wouldn't talk about it. "When I heard the news . . . I was completely devastated," she says. "It took me a week or so just to say [acute lymphocytic leukemia]. I wouldn't answer the phone. I just stayed in bed with a pillow over my head."

However, within a week, Shelley pulled herself together, determined to fight. She learned that the cure rate for this form of leukemia was between 65 and 75 percent. If she could survive only five more years, her chances of living a long and healthy life would soar to 95 percent.

Almost immediately, in October 1981, Shelley checked into New York City's Memorial Sloan-

Kettering Cancer Center, one of the world's leading cancer treatment facilities. There, medical specialists prescribed chemotherapy to attack the leukemia.

After six weeks of hospitalization, Shelley went into remission. Upon release from the hospital, she became an outpatient and continued on chemotherapy for two more years. She believes that the early diagnosis made all the difference in the final outcome of her case.

Restored to health, Shelley went on with her life. In the spring of 1983, she received the American Cancer Society's National Cancer Courage Award. The society cited her "for personal courage in her battle against cancer and . . . the hope and inspiration she gives all Americans in the fight for life and health."

Shelley believes it's impossible not to be changed by cancer. "You don't know what amazing inner strength you have until you're tested."

NAMAU'U MANOUA-KAINOA NEEDHAM

Illness can sometimes bring a community together. Seven-year-old Namau'u Manoua-Kainoa Needham found that out when he was diagnosed with acute myelogenous leukemia in September 1991. He lived in the tiny town of Hana in a remote part of the Hawaiian island of Maui. Dealing with leukemia was difficult for Namau'u and his family. Hana is connected to the rest of Maui by a narrow, twisting, treacherous, 23-mile-long road. Residents brag when they can drive the road in less than two hours. The town has only a small medical clinic, which is not equipped to treat leukemia cases. In addition, the Needham family did not have enough money to pay the huge medical bills that Namau'u would soon be receiving.

But the people of Hana came together to help Namau'u. Some people in town planned a large benefit concert at which the singer-actor Kris Kristofferson donated his talents. Through the sales and donations, the townspeople raised more than $12,000 for Namau'u's medical bills. They were also able to convince the Hawaiian Blood Bank to send a mobile unit to Hana to take blood donations. That trip is one the blood bank does not make often!

The people of Hana volunteered to donate blood, to work at the mobile unit, to transport blood to the airport, to serve refreshments, and to help in other ways. The blood donated was used to replace the more than three dozen units of blood that Namau'u had already received as treatment for his disease.

On January 6, 1992, Namau'u received a bone marrow transplant at Kaiser Permanente Hospital in Los Angeles, California. The donor was his thirteen-year-old brother, Kimo, whose blood turned out to be a good match for Namau'u's.

Namau'u's battle with leukemia was not over on January 6. But his brave fight shows how a community can band together to help one of its own members.

MAUREEN S.

Bone marrow transplants have led to many leukemia cures since Brooke Ward's success. Such procedures are particularly exciting when they take place between two unrelated individuals, as occurred with Brooke. This is what happened also with Maureen S. Maureen was not too discouraged when she was told that she had leukemia and that her only chance for survival depended on a bone marrow transplant. She had four sisters and two brothers and felt certain that someone in her family would be able to act as a donor.

But none had tissue types that matched hers. Nor could tissue matches be found among the 30,000 potential donors listed at the University of Minnesota. Maureen began to lose hope.

But her husband, Michael, did not give up. In a frenzied search, he turned to European bone marrow banks. He finally had success at the largest of these banks, Anthony Nolan Laboratories in England. Among the 70,000 potential donors listed there, one matched Maureen's tissue type.

The potential donor's name was Arthur S. Five years earlier, he had been tissue-typed during a blood donation. When Michael called to ask if Arthur would donate his marrow, the answer was a resounding yes. Someone Mr. S. knew had recently died of leukemia, and this opportunity seemed like a heaven-sent chance to memorialize his friend. "I felt privileged that I could help," he said. "Not many people are given this opportunity."

Arthur flew to Minnesota immediately, a bit nervous because this was his first plane trip. For several days, Maureen received large doses of chemotherapy and radiation to destroy her diseased bone marrow. At last the transplant took place. Ten days later, Maureen's white blood cell count slowly started to rise. The donor's marrow had begun to produce new blood cells.

Before Mr. S. returned to England, he went to say good-bye to Maureen. Maureen looked at him and started to cry. "This wonderful man, who hadn't known I existed until recently, had given me one last chance to see my children grow up," she explained.

After three months of hospitalization, Maureen went home. There has been no sign of relapse, and she has gone on with her life. What's more, she continues a warm friendship with Arthur S. They write each other every few months and exchange Christmas gifts. "That dear, generous man," she says. "I really owe him my life." She says she will never lose touch with him.

THE FAMILY DEALS WITH LEUKEMIA

As with many diseases, leukemia affects people besides the patient. The lives of family members also begin to change after diagnosis. Probably the first reactions to a diagnosis of leukemia are emotional responses. Patients are frightened, angry, confused, upset, and embarrassed. But so are family members. News that a family member has leukemia can produce emotional turmoil in a home.

For example, when children or teenagers become leukemia patients, their parents may feel worried, scared, tired, and confused by all the decisions they have to make. Caring for a leukemia patient of any age can be time-consuming and energy-draining. Family members may have to spend many hours at a hospital and many more hours caring for the patient at home. Many parents may feel they just don't have the energy to do everything that has to be done.

Family members may end up lashing out at others. After spending all day at the hospital with her sick daughter, a mother may come home and yell at her other children. The children may get upset and

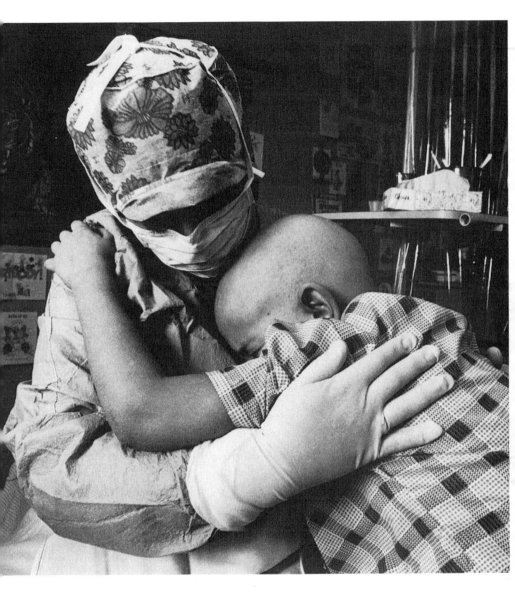

*Patients are frightened, angry, confused, and upset.
This young patient's mother comforts her son as best
she can, even though he may not come in contact with
her above the shoulders as this area is considered unsterile.*

resent their sick sister. And the mother may be even more upset when she realizes how she has reacted.

Children may also become angry at a sick parent. They may not understand why the parent can no longer spend time with them. They may even wonder if they did something wrong to lose the parent's love and attention.

Finances can be a problem too. Leukemia treatments can be very expensive. Some families may not be able to afford to pay for all the care needed. Arguments over money can tear family members apart.

Sometimes, however, this kind of crisis can draw a family closer together. For example, parents may begin spending more time with healthy children in the family to remind them that they are still loved and important. Children may recognize the pain and fear their parents are dealing with and offer their own support. Everyone works together to help the patient deal with his or her disease.

Medical and professional organizations work with leukemia patients and their families to help them learn how to live successfully with the disease. The Leukemia Society of America and its local chapters, for example, offer a variety of programs to help people deal with the emotional and financial problems created by leukemia. The Candlelighters Foundation is an international organization consisting of parents of young cancer patients. It has chapters in every state of the union and in ten foreign countries. Candlelighters publishes informational newsletters and booklets, provides speakers on every aspect of leukemia, and conducts meetings at which parents of leukemia patients can share their thoughts, feelings, and experiences. For countless families, it has been a beacon of hope in their battle against leukemia.

6
NEW HORIZONS IN RESEARCH ON LEUKEMIA

In 1972, Dr. Sidney L. Werkman wrote a touching and beautiful book about his wife's leukemia. "One brief look at a little drop of her blood," he said, "showed me that her illness was final, inexorable, hopeless." Sandy Werkman was diagnosed with acute myelogenous leukemia. Eight months later, Mrs. Werkman was dead of the disease.

In 1972, the chances of surviving acute myelogenous leukemia were so small that many physicians recommended that patients not even be treated. What a difference twenty years can make! In 1992, about 60 to 70 percent of all acute myelogenous leukemia patients experienced remission of their disease. Some have been cured, and many will go on to live healthy lives for a number of years. What further changes can we expect in the next twenty years?

Scientists are concentrating on four approaches to the treatment of leukemia. They are (1) basic research, (2) genetic engineering, (3) improved techniques for bone marrow transplantation, and (4) new chemicals.

BASIC RESEARCH

Scientists are constantly trying to learn more about the fundamental nature of the human body. They want to know more about such basic questions as how the human immune system works, what causes that system to break down, and how cancer cells develop. We can never hope to solve practical problems about leukemia until we answer basic questions such as these.

As just one example, many cancer researchers are now studying *oncogenes*, the medical term for "cancer genes." Oncogenes start out as normal genes with important functions during the early stages of human growth. At some point later in life, these genes become very active, and they reproduce rapidly in a way characteristic of cancer cells. Scientists believe that cancer-causing substances, such as benzene or radiation, may stimulate oncogenes to become potentially or actually malignant.

No one knows yet how or when this transformation occurs. Medical investigators are trying to narrow down the possible answers to those questions. They are working toward a greater understanding of oncogenes that might be used in both treatment and prevention of leukemia.

Research is being carried on at different centers in the expectation that, by identifying and understanding these special cancer genes, people who might be considered at risk can be singled out long before leukemia actually begins. The hope continues that eventually scientists can find a way to block the action of an oncogene and prevent or limit the growth of the leukemia that may result. This objective is probably a long way down the road. However, the exciting discovery of oncogenes has resulted in new and basic studies of cancer.

GENETIC ENGINEERING

Research on oncogenes also leads in another direction. Suppose that a scientist locates a mistake in a person's gene structure that has been shown to lead to leukemia. An attempt can be made, then, to remove the incorrect gene and replace it with the correct version.

Twenty years ago, that treatment was only a dream: no one knew how to change a person's gene structure. Today, scientists are moving toward a solution to that problem. A technique known as *genetic engineering* (or recombinant DNA) can be used to remove genes from or add genes to an organism's DNA, the hereditary material in our cells. That kind of genetic engineering has been used extensively and successfully with lower organisms, such as rats, pigs, and cows. In 1991 the first human trials with genetic engineering were begun. By 1992 about a dozen more human trials had been approved by the U.S. National Institutes of Health. Success in these trials could mean that genetic engineering will become a powerful tool in the battle against leukemia.

Genetic engineering is already being used in a second and totally different way in the fight against leukemia: in the development and manufacture of new antileukemic drugs. One of the drugs that has been found effective against chronic myelogenous leukemia is interferon. Interferon is a chemical that occurs naturally in the body, where it seems to have a number of functions.

Research suggests that interferon slows the growth of abnormal white blood cells and stimulates the body's own immune system. In some studies the combination of interferon with conventional drugs has been even more effective than the use of either by itself. The problem is that interferon is very difficult to obtain from natural sources, and there has been little to use in research and treatment.

Recently, however, researchers have found a way to make interferon by genetic engineering techniques. They insert into bacteria the gene that tells a cell how to make interferon. Then they allow the bacteria to live in a warm "soup" filled with food. As the bacteria grow and reproduce, they "read" the interferon gene along with all the other genes in their cells. They produce interferon, which scientists can filter out of the bacterial "soup."

IMPROVED TECHNIQUES FOR BONE MARROW TRANSPLANTATION

Scientists are constantly looking for ways to improve bone marrow transplants. Ideally, they would like to find ways of reducing the massive doses of chemotherapy and radiation therapy used in the early stages of bone marrow transplantation. At the same time, they are looking for new drugs or new ways of administering existing drugs in order to kill off the last few abnormal cells remaining in bone marrow before a transplant is conducted. Interferon has shown some promise for this application.

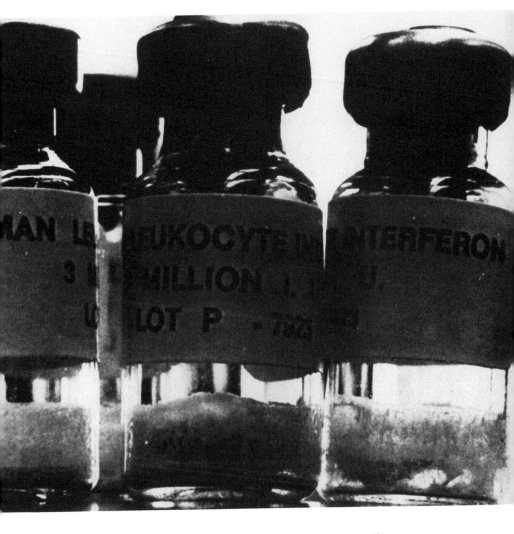

Researchers have recently found a way to genetically engineer interferon, a drug that has been found effective in the treatment of chronic myelogenous leukemia. Interferon occurs naturally in the body, and research suggests that it slows the growth of abnormal white blood cells and stimulates the body's own immune system.

Probably the single biggest problem with current bone marrow transplantation procedures is graft-versus-host disease. To deal with this problem, researchers are testing a number of new drugs that reduce the risk of that condition.

An exciting application of this research is the development of *nonfamilial transplants*. That term refers to the use of donors whose cells would traditionally be considered too different from those of the patient. If a way can be found to control graft-versus-host disease in nonfamilial transplants, the number of potential bone marrow donors will be greatly increased.

A three-year study on the use of nonfamilial transplants was completed at the University of Minnesota in 1988. In that study, transplants from nonrelatives and from relatives appeared to be about equally successful. Researchers predicted that survival rates would be about the same for the two groups of patients.

NEW CHEMICALS

A great deal of research effort is being devoted to finding new drugs to use against leukemia and more effective ways of administering them. At the present time, about two dozen drugs are available for use against leukemia.

Existing antileukemic drugs can be classified into three major groups: (1) cell toxins, (2) wedge chemicals, and (3) biological response modifiers. Cell toxins destroy abnormal (as well as normal) cells. Wedge chemicals are compounds that prevent the growth and/or reproduction of cancerous cells. Biological response modifiers are compounds with two distinct effects: first, they stimulate the immune system to destroy malignant cells; second, they encourage malignant cells to mature and become normal.

As for finding new drugs that can be used against leukemia, one promising product of that current research is 2-chlorodeoxyadenosine, a chemical designed for use against hairy-cell leukemia. This form of leukemia is characterized by changes in the appearance of white blood cells in the bone marrow. From smooth-looking infection fighters, the cells become abnormal and grow what look like hairy tentacles.

In a recent study, twelve patients were given small doses of 2-chlorodeoxyadenosine for a week. At the end of that period, eleven went into remission. To date the average remission has remained after eighteen months. In one patient there has been no sign of leukemia cells for four years.

The chemical 2-chlorodeoxyadenosine is an example of a designer drug. In producing a designer drug, a chemist sets out to manufacture a chemical molecule that has certain specific characteristics. The molecule might be similar to that of an existing drug. But the chemist makes a slight change in the molecule in an attempt to avoid side effects resulting from the first drug's use.

Scientists also continue to explore the use of drug combinations, in which two or more drugs are used together. For example, Dr. Donald Miller at the University of Alabama in Birmingham has had success in treating chronic myelogenous leukemia with a combination of a new drug, mithramycin, and a standard antileukemic drug, hydroxyurea. Six out of nine patients showed dramatic improvement with the combination drug therapy.

A somewhat different approach to chemotherapy involves monitoring a patient's body responses to drugs. Researchers have long been aware that in some patients malignant cells have a frustrating ability to become resistant to the effects of various drugs. It is this characteristic of malignant cells that causes certain leukemias not to respond to chemotherapy or to recur after seemingly successful treatment.

This phenomenon has led some researchers to examine the genetic basis for an individual leukemia patient's ability to respond to chemotherapy or to be resistant to it. Doctors know that solving the problem of why different patients respond differently to antileukemic drugs will remove one more barrier to effective prolonged response to those drugs. Then they will be able to design more effective chemotherapies.

Kevin Scanlon, a Leukemia Society of America biochemist at the City of Hope National Medical Center in Duarte, California, has developed a simple test that can analyze a patient's DNA. The test detects changes in the DNA that indicate whether the patient's leukemia has become resistant to chemotherapy.

The Scanlon test would improve the use of chemotherapy by enabling doctors to pinpoint the moment when a patient becomes resistant to treatment. At that point, the patient can be switched to different drugs. In short, specialists expect the test to allow drugs to be changed at the proper time to improve therapy.

Leukemia research pursues a variety of pathways. But all are aimed at finding mechanisms for stopping the growth of abnormal white blood cells and encouraging the growth of new, healthy blood cells in the patient's body. Therein lies the hope for remission and, eventually, cure of the disease.

7

LOOKING AHEAD

Researchers have come a long way from the days when the diagnosis of leukemia was a virtual death sentence. No one knew precisely when death would occur, but there was a certainty of life cut short.

Today, the struggle against leukemia continues. It is not possible to say when or how the battle will be won. But we do know that enormous progress has been made in the past three decades, including progress in

- Further understanding the causes of leukemia and related diseases

- Learning more about basic cell structure and how this knowledge applies to leukemia

- Treating the various forms of the disorder

- Achieving cures for an increasing number of cases, especially those among children

Looking ahead, the possibility exists that more and more patients will receive individualized therapy tailored to specific characteristics of their disease. It's even theoretically possible that scientists will find ways to turn off oncogenes in order to interrupt the cancer process before it can become destructive.

Without seeing the problem through rose-colored glasses, doctors view the future hopefully. They feel optimistic about greater success with extending and maintaining remissions to the five years past therapy which indicates cure. Bone marrow transplantation has moved beyond the experimental stage. The procedure has extended the lives of many patients and probably cured at least some of them. Research now includes further trials aimed at broadening the pool of suitable donors and improving autologous transplant techniques. Also on the research agenda is the search for new antileukemic drugs, chemicals that will destroy malignant cells and encourage the growth of normal ones.

Thus, the battle against leukemia and related diseases moves forward on a variety of fronts. Reports of progress excite patients and their families, researchers, and the general public.

A cure may be on the horizon. And even it if is still not in sight, researchers are making great strides in prolonging and improving the quality of patients' lives. The outlook for all leukemia patients continues to brighten.

It has not been easy to reach this point, and it will not be easy to finally overcome the disease. But most experts believe that—if current efforts continue—victory eventually will be achieved.

APPENDIX

ORGANIZATIONS

Candlelighters Foundation
1901 Pennsylvania Avenue, N.W.
Washington, DC 20006
202-659-5136

An international organization of and for parents of
young cancer patients. Supports self-help groups and
publishes a newsletter and lists of reading materials
for members and for medical and social work profes-
sionals.

The Leukemia Society of America, Inc.
600 Third Avenue
New York, NY 10016
212-573-8484 or
800-955-4LSA

Supports research on leukemia, patient assistance,
and professional and public education. Provides
pamphlets on the disease and offers financial assistance for disease-related expenses. Has fifty-seven
local offices in thirty-three states.

The National Cancer Institute
Office of Cancer Communications
Bethesda, MD 20892
800-4-CANCER

Publishes books and pamphlets about various forms of cancer and the work of the National Cancer Institute.

GLOSSARY

acute: developing quickly, with severe symptoms, and lasting a relatively brief period of time. The opposite of **chronic.**

antigen: any substance that enters the body and stimulates a response from the immune system.

autologous transplant: a bone marrow transplant that uses a patient's own bone marrow, taken while he or she is still relatively healthy.

chemotherapy: treatment with drugs.

chronic: developing slowly, over a long period of time, with relatively mild symptoms early in the disease; the opposite of **acute.**

genetic engineering: any procedure by which scientists change an organism's genetic makeup, for example, to treat some disorder.

graft-versus-host disease: a dangerous reaction between the cells of grafted tissue and host tissue, especially when the host's immune system is depressed.

granulocyte: a type of white blood cell that destroys microorganisms by digesting them; basophils, eosinophils, mast cells, and neutrophils are examples of granulocytes.

granulocytic leukemia: a form of leukemia that develops when granulocytes reproduce at an abnormally rapid rate.

high-level radiation: a nonspecific term that refers to levels of radiation that result in serious health problems in a relatively short period of time.

host cell: in transplants, a host cell is one that comes from the patient, the person who receives the transplant.

interferon: a chemical produced by a cell that has been infected that acts to prevent other cells from being infected.

leukemia: a form of cancer that originates in the blood-forming tissues of bone marrow, lymph nodes, and the spleen. The disease is characterized by the uncontrolled production of abnormal white cells.

leukocyte: a white blood cell; leukocytes are subdivided into three major groups: granulocytes, lymphocytes, and monocytes.

low-level radiation: a nonspecific term that refers to levels of radiation that do not produce immediate, serious health problems but that may result in such problems later in life.

lymphocyte: white blood cells that kill disease organisms that enter the body.

lymphocytic leukemia: a form of leukemia that develops when lymphocytes reproduce at an abnormally rapid rate.

myelocytic (or myelogenous) leukemia: a form of leukemia that develops when granulocytes reproduce at an abnormally rapid rate; see also **granulocytic leukemia.**

nonfamilial transplant: a bone marrow transplant between two unrelated individuals who might normally be considered incompatible for a transplant.

oncogene: a gene that occurs normally in the body and has normal functions for much of a person's life, but that at some point becomes overactive, producing cancer cells.

relapse: the reappearance of a disease after its symptoms had disappeared for some period of time.

remission: the disappearance of the symptoms of a disease; a remission can be either temporary or permanent.

FOR FURTHER READING

Adams, David W., and Eleanor Deveau. *Coping with Childhood Cancer*. Reston, Va.: Reston, 1984.

Alsop, Stewart. *Stay of Execution*. Philadelphia: Lippincott, 1973.

Baker, Lynn. *You and Leukemia*. Philadelphia: Saunders, 1988.

Bombeck, Erma. *I Want to Grow Hair, I Want to Grow Up, I Want to Go to Boise*. New York: Harper & Row, 1989.

Bracken, Jeanne. *Children with Cancer: A Comprehensive Reference Guide for Parents*. New York: Oxford, 1986.

Ekert, Henry. *Childhood Cancer: Understanding and Coping*. New York: Gordon and Breach, 1989.

Herda, D. J. *Cancer*. New York: Franklin Watts, 1989.

Holleb, Arthur I., ed. *The American Cancer Society Cancer Book*. Garden City, N.Y.: Doubleday, 1989.

Laszlo, John. *Understanding Cancer*. New York: Harper & Row, 1987.

Lax, Eric. *Life and Death on 10 West*. New York: Times Books, 1984.

Lund, Doris. *Eric*. New York: Dell, 1976.

Mann, Bruce W. *Leukemia: A Family's Challenge.* Traverse City, Mich.: Prism, 1987.

Margolies, Cynthia P., and Kenneth B. McCredie. *Understanding Leukemia.* New York: Scribner, 1983.

Pendleton, Edith. *Too Old to Cry . . . Too Young to Die.* Nashville, Tenn.: Thomas Nelson, 1980.

Schulz, Charles. *Why Charlie Brown, Why?* New York: St. Martin's, 1990.

Spinetta, John J., and Patricia Deasy-Spinetta. *Emotional Aspects of Childhood Leukemia.* New York: Leukemia Society of America, 1991.

Tucker, Jonathan B. *Ellie: A Child's Fight against Leukemia.* New York: Holt, Rinehart, 1982.

Werkman, Sidney L. *A Little Time.* Boston: Little, Brown, 1972.

PAMPHLETS

Acute Lymphocytic Leukemia. Leukemia Society of America, P-33 40M, 1991.

Acute Myelogenous Leukemia. Leukemia Society of America, P-32 20M, 1991.

Bone Marrow Transplantation: Questions & Answers. Leukemia Society of America, P-15 50M, 1989.

Cancer Facts and Figures—1990. American Cancer Society, 90-425M-No.5008-LE, 1990.

Chronic Lymphocytic Leukemia. Leukemia Society of America, P-34 10M, 1991.

Chronic Myelogenous Leukemia. Leukemia Society of America, P-31 40M, 1991.

Coping with Survival. Leukemia Society of America, P-35 50M, 1990.

Emotional Aspects of Childhood Leukemia. Leukemia Society of America, P-14 15M, 1991.

Leukemia: Research Report. U.S. Department of Health and Human Services, 88-329, 1987.

Radiation Therapy and You: A Guide to Self-Help During Treatment. U.S. Department of Health and Human Services, 88-2227, 1987.

Understanding Chemotherapy. Leukemia Society of America, P-36 20M, 1991.

What Everyone Should Know about Leukemia. Leukemia Society of America, P-9 115M, 1991.

What Happened to You Happened to Me. American Cancer Society, 84-10M-No.4546-PS, 1984.

What it is that I have, don't want, didn't ask for, can't give back, and how I feel about it. Leukemia Society of America, P-16 10M, 1991.

When Someone in Your Family Has Cancer. U.S. Department of Health and Human Services, NIH Publication 88-2685, 1987.

When Your Brother or Sister Has Cancer. American Cancer Society, 84-10M-No.4510-PS, 1984.

INDEX